Powerful Words

of Jesus

Life Changing Truth

Dr. R.D. Manning

"Powerful Words of Jesus: Life Changing Truth"

Dr. R.D. Manning - Author

Copyright © 2024 by R.D. Manning

All rights reserved.

ISBN:

Interactive Faith Ministries

P.O. Box 1615

Williamston, N.C. 27892

U.S.A

revrickmanning@gmail.com

Interactivefaith.org

No part of this publication may be reproduced, stored in a retrieval system, or transmitted, in any form or by any means, electronic, mechanical, photocopying, recording, or otherwise, without the prior written permission of the publisher, except for brief quotations in critical reviews or articles.

First Edition: 2024

Table of Contents

Introduction 1

Chapter 1: "Follow Me": The Call to Discipleship 4

Chapter 2: "Love One Another": The Greatest Commandment 11

Chapter 3: "I Am the Bread of Life": Finding True Satisfaction 19

Chapter 4: "It Is Finished": The Victory of the Cross 27

Chapter 5: "Take Up Your Cross": The Cost of Commitment 35

Chapter 6: "Peace Be Still": Power Over Life's Storms 44

Chapter 7: "I Am the Light of the World": Walking in His Truth 52

Chapter 8: "Let Not Your Heart Be Troubled": Hope for Troubled Times 59

Chapter 9: "Come Unto Me": Finding Rest in Jesus 66

Chapter 10: "I Am the Resurrection and the Life": The Promise of Eternity 73

Chapter 11: "Go Ye Therefore": The Great Commission......... 80

Chapter 12: "Lo, I Am with You Always": The Promise of His Presence 87

Chapter 13: "Thy Sins Be Forgiven Thee": The Power of Mercy 94

Chapter 14: "Ask, and It Shall Be Given": Bold Faith in Prayer 100

Chapter 15: "I Am the True Vine": Staying Connected to Christ 107

Introduction

Introduction

Have you ever heard words so powerful they stopped you in your tracks? Words that seemed to go straight to your heart, cutting through all the noise of life and speaking directly to your deepest needs? The words of Jesus Christ are like that. They aren't just historical quotes or religious phrases—they're alive. They carry power, truth, and the ability to completely change your life.

When Jesus spoke, things happened. The blind could see. The dead came back to life. Storms stopped raging. But His words weren't just for the people in Bible times. They're for us, too—for you, right here, right now. He said, "Come unto me, all ye that labour and are heavy laden, and I will give you rest" (Matthew 11:28, KJV). Doesn't that sound like exactly what we all need? Rest. Peace. Hope.

This book isn't about just reading what Jesus said. It's about understanding how His words apply to your life today. His words offer more than comfort; they're an invitation. An invitation to let go of your burdens, to find strength in Him, and to discover a life full of purpose and joy.

In the chapters ahead, we'll take a closer look at some of the most powerful things Jesus ever said. Each chapter unpacks one of His life-changing statements, showing how His words can heal your heart, give you direction, and bring you closer to God. Whether you're struggling with fear, searching for answers, or just trying to find your way, His words have the power to meet you where you are.

But there's a question only you can answer: Will you listen? Jesus didn't speak just to be heard. He spoke so that people would believe and take action. His words invite us to trust Him, to walk in faith, and to experience the incredible blessings He's promised.

Maybe you've heard these words before but never really let them sink in. Or maybe this is the first time you're hearing that Jesus has something to say to you personally. Either way, my prayer is that as you read, you'll discover just how much these words can change everything.

The words of Jesus are eternal. He said, "Heaven and earth shall pass away, but my words shall not pass away" (Matthew 24:35, KJV). That means they'll never lose their power, their relevance, or their truth. His words are just as powerful today as when He first spoke them.

So, are you ready to hear them? Are you ready to let them change your life? As you turn the pages of this book, open your heart to what Jesus is saying. I promise, His words have the power to bring peace, joy, and hope like nothing else in this world.

Let's begin this journey together, exploring the most powerful words of Jesus Christ—and discovering how they can transform your life forever.

Chapter 1:

"Follow Me": The Call to Discipleship

The Call That Changes Everything

"**Follow me.**" Two simple words. Yet, these words, spoken by Jesus Christ, carry an eternal weight that has transformed lives, shaped destinies, and altered the course of human history. The call to follow Jesus is not a mere invitation. But it is a command that requires obedience, commitment, and faith.

Through the lens of scripture, we'll examine the profound personal value that comes from obedience to His Word. Obedience is not just a duty; it is the key to experiencing abundant life, peace, and purpose. Jesus does not call us to follow Him into ambiguity or uncertainty but into a life of eternal significance.

As we embark on this journey, we will see how the call to follow Jesus impacts not only our relationship with God but also how we live, think, and interact with the world around us.

What Does It Mean to "Follow Me"?

When Jesus called His first disciples, He said, *"Follow me, and I will make you fishers of men"* (Matthew 4:19, KJV). With these words, He set the foundation for what it means to follow Him.

1. **A Call to Relationship**

    The call to follow Jesus is first and foremost a call to relationship. Jesus did not ask Peter, Andrew, James, or John to complete a checklist of religious duties; He asked them to walk with Him. In John 15:15, Jesus said, *"I have called you friends.*" He desires intimacy with His disciples, not mere compliance.

Illustration: Picture a shepherd leading his sheep. The sheep follow not because they understand the destination but because they trust the shepherd's voice (John 10:27). Following Jesus is about trusting Him, even when we don't see the full picture.

2. **A Call to Obedience**

This is the cornerstone of discipleship. In Luke 5:5, Peter demonstrated this when Jesus told him to cast his nets after a long night of catching nothing. Peter replied, *"Nevertheless at thy word I will let down the net."* His obedience led to an overwhelming blessing; a catch so large it threatened to break the nets.

Wisdom Key: Obedience to God's Word opens the door to divine provision and miracles.

3. **A Call to Surrender**

Following Jesus requires surrendering our will, plans, and desires to His lordship. In Luke 9:23, Jesus said, *"If any man will come after me, let him deny himself, and take up his cross daily, and follow me."* This is not a passive act but an intentional daily decision to place Christ above all else.

Example: When the rich young ruler encountered Jesus, he was invited to follow Him. However, he walked away sorrowful because he was unwilling to surrender his possessions (Matthew 19:21-22). This story illustrates that following Jesus demands prioritizing Him above earthly treasures.

Application: The Rewards of Obedience

Obedience to Jesus is not without reward. While the journey of discipleship requires sacrifice, it also brings unparalleled blessings.

1. **Personal Transformation**

   In Matthew 16:24-25, Jesus said, *"For whosoever will save his life shall lose it: and whosoever will lose his life for my sake shall find it."* Obedience to Christ leads to a transformation of the heart and mind.

   Testimony: Consider the transformation of Saul into Paul. Once a persecutor of Christians, Paul became one of the greatest apostles because he obeyed Jesus' call on the road to Damascus (Acts 9:1-22).

   Action Step: Reflect on areas of your life where God is calling you to surrender and trust Him. Write them down and commit to praying for strength to obey.

2. **Divine Purpose**

   When Jesus called His disciples, He promised to make them fishers of men (Matthew 4:19). This signifies that following Jesus aligns us with His divine purpose.

Wisdom Key: God's purpose for your life is discovered in the place of obedience.

Example: Moses experienced God's purpose when he obeyed His command to lead Israel out of Egypt. Though Moses doubted his abilities, God equipped him for the task.

3. **Eternal Rewards**

Following Jesus has eternal significance. In John 14:2-3, Jesus assured His disciples, *"I go to prepare a place for you."* Obedience to His call secures our eternal home with Him.

Illustration: Imagine a child trusting their parent to lead them home. The child doesn't worry about the path because they trust the one guiding them. Similarly, we can trust Jesus to lead us to our heavenly destination.

How to Follow Jesus Today

1. **Hear His Voice**

    - Read the Word of God daily (Romans 10:17).

    - Spend time in prayer to discern His will.

2. **Obey His Commands**

    - Apply what you read in scripture to your life (James 1:22).

    - Trust His guidance even when it challenges your understanding.

3. **Surrender Completely**
   - Lay down your plans and ambitions at His feet (Proverbs 3:5-6).
   - Make following Him your highest priority.

4. **Stay Committed**
   - Persevere through trials, knowing they produce growth (James 1:2-4).
   - Surround yourself with a community of believers for encouragement and accountability.

Closing Prayer

Heavenly Father,

We thank You for the call of Jesus to follow Him. Help us to trust Your voice, obey Your Word, and surrender our lives completely to You. Strengthen us in our daily walk, and remind us of the eternal rewards that come from obedience. May we always seek to glorify You in all that we do. In Jesus' name, we pray. Amen.

Chapter Summary

The call to follow Jesus is not just an invitation; it is a divine command that transforms lives. By embracing relationship, obedience, and surrender, we align ourselves with God's purpose and experience His blessings. Through obedience, we find true personal value and eternal significance.

Wisdom Keys:

- Obedience to Jesus unlocks divine provision.
- God's purpose is discovered in the place of surrender.
- The journey of discipleship leads to eternal rewards.

This chapter serves as a foundation for understanding the most powerful words of Jesus and how they call us into a life of faith, obedience, and purpose.

Chapter 2:

"Love One Another":

The Greatest Commandment

"Love One Another": The Greatest Commandment

The Power of Love in Action

When Jesus was asked to identify the greatest commandment in the law, His response was both profound and transformative: *"Thou shalt love the Lord thy God with all thy heart, and with all thy soul, and with all thy mind. This is the first and great commandment. And the second is like unto it, Thou shalt love thy neighbour as thyself"* (Matthew 22:37-39, KJV).

The essence of Christ's teaching rests on love—love for God and love for one another. This chapter explores the profound call to "love one another," its implications for daily living, and the spiritual transformation it brings when we obey this command. Love is not merely an emotion; it is a choice, an action, and the foundation of the Christian life.

In this chapter, you'll learn the true personal value of walking in love and staying sweet in your attitude toward others, even in challenging circumstances. By following Jesus' example, we can cultivate a love that reflects His heart and draws others to Him.

Understanding the Greatest Commandment

1. **What Does It Mean to Love One Another?**

    The love Jesus speaks of is *agape* love—a selfless, unconditional love that seeks the best for others. It is not dependent on feelings or circumstances but is a deliberate choice to act with kindness, compassion, and humility.

- *"By this shall all men know that ye are my disciples, if ye have love one to another"* (John 13:35, KJV).
- Loving one another is a reflection of our relationship with Christ. It is the evidence of true discipleship.

Illustration: Consider the Good Samaritan (Luke 10:25-37). While others passed by the wounded man, the Samaritan demonstrated agape love by showing compassion and meeting his needs. This parable highlights the importance of loving not just in words but in actions.

Wisdom Key: Love is not just something you feel; it is something you do.

2. **Why Is Love the Greatest Commandment?**

    - **It Fulfills the Law:** *"Love worketh no ill to his neighbour: therefore love is the fulfilling of the law"* (Romans 13:10, KJV).

    Love encapsulates all other commandments because it seeks the good of others.

    - **It Reflects God's Character:** *"God is love"* (1 John 4:8, KJV). When we love, we mirror God's nature and demonstrate His presence in our lives.

    Example: Jesus washing His disciples' feet (John 13:4-17) is a powerful illustration of love in action. He, the Master, humbled Himself to serve, setting an example of selfless love for us to follow.

Application: Walking in Love Daily

1. **How to Cultivate a Heart of Love**

   - **Spend Time with God:** Love flows from our relationship with Him. The more time we spend in His presence, the more His love will overflow in our lives.
     - *"We love him, because he first loved us"* (1 John 4:19, KJV).
   - **Meditate on the Word:** Scripture renews our minds and teaches us how to love. Memorize verses like 1 Corinthians 13:4-7 to keep love at the forefront of your thoughts.

   Action Step: Start each day by asking God to help you see others through His eyes and to fill your heart with His love.

2. **Staying Sweet in Your Attitudes**

   - **Guard Your Heart:** *"Keep thy heart with all diligence; for out of it are the issues of life"* (Proverbs 4:23, KJV). Negative attitudes often stem from unresolved hurts or bitterness. Surrender these to God.

- **Choose Forgiveness:** Holding onto offenses poisons your spirit. Jesus said, *"Forgive, and ye shall be forgiven"* (Luke 6:37, KJV).

  Example: Stephen, the first Christian martyr, demonstrated incredible love when he prayed for those stoning him: *"Lord, lay not this sin to their charge"* (Acts 7:60, KJV).

  Wisdom Key: Staying sweet in your attitude requires daily surrender to God's grace and the willingness to forgive.

3. **Practical Steps for Walking in Love**

   - **Listen More, Speak Less:** *"Let every man be swift to hear, slow to speak, slow to wrath"* (James 1:19, KJV). Listening shows respect and care for others.

   - **Serve Others:** Look for ways to meet the needs of those around you, just as Jesus did.

   - **Pray for Others:** Prayer softens your heart and aligns you with God's love for them.

The Impact of Loving One Another

1. **It Strengthens Relationships**

   Love builds trust and fosters unity. When we prioritize love, we create an environment where relationships can flourish.

   Example: Ruth's devotion to Naomi (Ruth 1:16-17) exemplifies love that strengthens bonds. Ruth's commitment to Naomi, even in hardship, reflects the beauty of selfless love.

2. **It Draws Others to Christ**

Jesus said, *"Let your light so shine before men, that they may see your good works, and glorify your Father which is in heaven"* (Matthew 5:16, KJV). Our love for others is a powerful testimony that can lead people to Christ.

Testimony: A believer's consistent kindness and love in the workplace can open doors for sharing the gospel with coworkers.

3. **It Transforms Your Life**

When you choose to love, you experience the joy, peace, and fulfillment that come from living in alignment with God's will.

Wisdom Key: Love is a seed; when you sow it, you reap a harvest of blessing in your own life.

Staying Committed to Love

Walking in love is not always easy. There will be times when people test your patience or challenge your ability to forgive. However, Jesus never said it would be easy—He said it would be worth it.

1. **Look to Jesus as Your Example**

   "Looking unto Jesus the author and finisher of our faith" (Hebrews 12:2, KJV). Jesus loved unconditionally, even in the face of rejection and suffering.

2. **Rely on the Holy Spirit**

   The Holy Spirit empowers us to love beyond our natural abilities. *"The love of God is shed abroad in our hearts by the Holy Ghost which is given unto us"* (Romans 5:5, KJV).

Closing Prayer

Heavenly Father,

We thank You for the incredible gift of Your love. Help us to love You with all our heart, soul, and mind and to love others as You have commanded. Teach us to walk in love daily, to forgive freely, and to stay sweet in our attitudes toward those around us. Empower us through Your Holy Spirit to reflect Your love in every aspect of our lives. May our love be a testimony of Your grace and truth, drawing others to You. In Jesus' name, we pray. Amen.

Chapter Summary

The command to "love one another" is central to the Christian life. It reflects God's nature, fulfills His law, and transforms our relationships and our own hearts. By walking in love and staying sweet in our attitudes, we not only honor God but also draw others to Him.

Wisdom Keys:

- Love is not just an emotion; it's a choice to act in kindness and compassion.

- Staying sweet in your attitude requires guarding your heart and choosing forgiveness.

- Walking in love transforms your life and strengthens your witness for Christ.

Chapter 3:

"I Am the Bread of Life": Finding True Satisfaction

The Search for True Fulfillment

In every human heart is a deep longing for meaning and fulfillment. People seek satisfaction in careers, relationships, material possessions, and personal achievements. Yet, despite their efforts, they often feel empty, restless, and unsatisfied. This search for fulfillment points to a truth that Jesus revealed: He is the only source of true satisfaction.

In John 6:35, Jesus declares, *"I am the bread of life: he that cometh to me shall never hunger; and he that believeth on me shall never thirst"* (KJV). With these powerful words, Jesus invites us to turn away from temporary solutions and come to Him for the eternal nourishment our souls desperately need.

This chapter explores how Christ, as the Bread of Life, satisfies our spiritual hunger, equips us to fulfill our divine purpose, and transforms our lives when we make Him our Lord and Savior. By the end, you will understand how to find true satisfaction in Jesus and align your life with God's divine plan.

Understanding "I Am the Bread of Life"

1. **The Context of Jesus' Declaration**

    In John 6, Jesus had just performed the miraculous feeding of the 5,000 with five loaves and two fish. The crowd was amazed but misunderstood the significance of the miracle.

They sought Jesus for physical bread, but He pointed them to a greater truth: the need for spiritual sustenance.

- *"Labour not for the meat which perisheth, but for that meat which endureth unto everlasting life, which the Son of man shall give unto you"* (John 6:27, KJV).
- Jesus wanted them to recognize that He was offering something far greater than physical food—He was offering eternal life.

Illustration: Just as physical bread sustains the body, Jesus, the Bread of Life, sustains the soul. A car runs on fuel, and when it's empty, it stops. Likewise, our souls are designed to run on the presence of God. Without Him, we are spiritually empty.

2. **The Meaning of "Bread of Life"** Bread in biblical times was a staple of life—essential, nourishing, and satisfying. By calling Himself the Bread of Life, Jesus declared that He is:

   - **Essential for Life:** Just as bread sustains physical life, Jesus sustains spiritual life.
   - **The Source of True Satisfaction:** Worldly pursuits may temporarily fill, but only Jesus can fully satisfy the deepest desires of the heart.
   - **Eternal Nourishment:** Physical bread perishes, but the life Jesus offers endures forever.

Wisdom Key: True fulfillment comes not from what you possess but from who possesses you.

Application: How Jesus Satisfies Our Deepest Needs

1. **He Satisfies Our Hunger for Meaning**

    o Every human being is created with a purpose. Ephesians 2:10 reminds us, *"For we are his workmanship, created in Christ Jesus unto good works, which God hath before ordained that we should walk in them"* (KJV).

    o Jesus satisfies our hunger for meaning by revealing God's plan for our lives and equipping us to fulfill it.

    Example: Consider the apostle Peter. Before following Jesus, Peter was a fisherman with a simple life. But Jesus called him to a greater purpose: *"Follow me, and I will make you fishers of men"* (Matthew 4:19, KJV). Peter's life was transformed as he found true meaning in Christ.

    Action Step: Spend time in prayer and study of God's Word to discover His purpose for your life.

2. **He Heals Our Inner Emptiness**

    o Many people feel an ache of emptiness that they try to fill with success, relationships, or distractions. But only Jesus can heal the void within.

- Psalm 107:9 declares, *"For he satisfieth the longing soul, and filleth the hungry soul with goodness"* (KJV).

Testimony: A man who spent years chasing wealth and fame finally gave his life to Christ and discovered the peace and joy he had been missing.

Wisdom Key: When Jesus is at the center of your life, everything else falls into place.

3. **He Provides Strength for Daily Living**

    - Just as bread provides energy for the body, Jesus gives us strength to face life's challenges. Philippians 4:13 reminds us, *"I can do all things through Christ which strengtheneth me"* (KJV).

    - When we partake of the Bread of Life through prayer, worship, and communion, we receive the spiritual strength we need.

    Action Step: Begin each day by feeding on God's Word and seeking His guidance.

Staying Connected to the Bread of Life

1. **Daily Dependence on Christ**

    - Jesus taught us to pray, *"Give us this day our daily bread"* (Matthew 6:11, KJV), reminding us of our constant need for Him.

- Dependence on Christ means prioritizing time with Him daily and trusting Him to meet your needs.

Illustration: Just as manna sustained the Israelites in the wilderness (Exodus 16), Jesus provides daily sustenance for our souls.

2. **Guarding Against Distractions**

    - The world offers many substitutes for true satisfaction, but they leave us empty.
    - Colossians 3:2 advises, *"Set your affection on things above, not on things on the earth"* (KJV). Keep your focus on Christ.

Wisdom Key: What you feed your soul determines your spiritual health. Feed it with God's Word, not the fleeting pleasures of the world.

The Promise of Eternal Life

1. **Believing in Jesus**

    - Jesus promises, *"He that believeth on me hath everlasting life"* (John 6:47, KJV).
    - True satisfaction begins with placing your faith in Christ and receiving the gift of salvation.

2. **Living with Eternity in Mind**

    - When we focus on Jesus, our perspective shifts from temporary concerns to eternal significance.

- Paul wrote, *"For to me to live is Christ, and to die is gain"* (Philippians 1:21, KJV).

Testimony: A believer facing terminal illness shared the peace and hope she found in Christ, inspiring others to trust Him.

Action Step: Reflect on how your daily choices align with eternal priorities.

Closing Prayer

Heavenly Father,

Thank You for sending Jesus, the Bread of Life, to satisfy our deepest hunger and give us eternal life. Help us to seek Him daily and to trust in His sufficiency for every need. May we find true satisfaction in His presence and live lives that fulfill Your divine purpose. Strengthen us to share this Bread with others so they too may experience the joy and peace that comes from knowing You. In Jesus' name, we pray. Amen.

Wisdom Keys and Action Steps

- **Wisdom Keys:**
  - True fulfillment comes not from what you possess but from who possesses you.
  - When Jesus is at the center of your life, everything else falls into place.

- What you feed your soul determines your spiritual health.

- **Action Steps:**
  - Spend time in prayer and study of God's Word daily.
  - Seek God's purpose for your life and align your actions with it.
  - Feed your soul with God's Word and worship, avoiding worldly distractions.

Chapter 4:

"It Is Finished": The Victory of the Cross

The Power of a Finished Work

In the final moments of Jesus' earthly life, hanging on the cross, He uttered the powerful words: *"It is finished"* (John 19:30, KJV). These words marked the culmination of His mission to redeem humanity. They were not words of defeat but of triumph, declaring the completion of His sacrificial work on the cross.

When Jesus said, *"It is finished,"* He announced the victory over sin, death, and the grave. He had paid the sin debt that humanity could never pay, fulfilling the divine plan of salvation. The impact of these words resonates throughout eternity, giving every believer access to the abundant life here on earth and the promise of eternal life in heaven.

This chapter will explore the victory of the cross and how it secures personal victory for every believer. By understanding the depth of what Jesus accomplished, you can walk confidently in the freedom, authority, and peace that His finished work provides.

What Did Jesus Finish on the Cross?

1. **The Fulfillment of Prophecy**

    The cross was not an accident but the fulfillment of God's plan for redemption, foretold throughout the Old Testament.

    - Isaiah 53:5 declares, *"But he was wounded for our transgressions, he was bruised for our iniquities: the chastisement* of our peace was upon him; and with his stripes we are healed"* (KJV).

- From the Passover lamb in Exodus to the promises of a Messiah in the Psalms and Prophets, the cross was always central to God's plan.

Illustration: Just as a builder completes a blueprint by laying every brick according to the plan, Jesus perfectly fulfilled the Father's will, ensuring every prophetic promise came to pass.

2. **The Payment for Sin**

   - Humanity's greatest problem is sin, which separates us from God. Romans 6:23 reminds us, *"For the wages of sin is death; but the gift of God is eternal life through Jesus Christ our Lord"* (KJV).

   - At the cross, Jesus bore the punishment for our sins, satisfying God's justice and making a way for forgiveness.

   Wisdom Key: The cross was not the end of Jesus' story; it was the beginning of ours.

3. **The Defeat of Satan and Death**

   - Through His sacrifice, Jesus disarmed the powers of darkness. Colossians 2:15 declares, *"And having spoiled principalities and powers, he made a shew of them openly, triumphing over them in it"* (KJV).

- The resurrection confirmed His victory, breaking the power of death and giving believers eternal life.

Testimony: Think of Paul's transformation—from a persecutor of the church to a bold preacher of the Gospel—powered by his faith in the victory of the cross.

Application: How the Victory of the Cross Affects Our Lives

1. **Freedom from Sin and Guilt**

   - Jesus' finished work sets us free from the power of sin. Romans 8:1 assures us, *"There is therefore now no condemnation to them which are in Christ Jesus"* (KJV).
   - Many believers carry guilt for past mistakes, but the cross offers full forgiveness.

   Illustration: Imagine a prisoner who has been declared free but chooses to remain in the cell. The cross opens the door—will you walk out?

   Action Step: Confess your sins to God, believe in His forgiveness, and release guilt to walk in freedom.

2. **Victory in Daily Living**

   - The cross empowers us to live victoriously over temptation, fear, and challenges.
   - Galatians 2:20 teaches, *"I am crucified with Christ: nevertheless I live; yet not I, but Christ liveth in me"* (KJV).

Wisdom Key: The victory of the cross is not just for eternity; it's for every moment of your life.

3. **Peace with God**
   - Jesus' sacrifice reconciles us to God, restoring a relationship broken by sin.
   - Ephesians 2:14 calls Him *"our peace"* (KJV). This peace surpasses circumstances and anchors us in God's love.

Practical Steps to Walk in the Victory of the Cross

1. **Believe and Receive**
   - Salvation begins with faith. John 3:16 reminds us, *"For God so loved the world, that he gave his only begotten Son, that whosoever believeth in him should not perish, but have everlasting life"* (KJV).
   - Accept Jesus as your Savior, and live in the assurance of His finished work.

2. **Renew Your Mind**
   - Romans 12:2 urges us, *"Be ye transformed by the renewing of your mind"* (KJV). Replace lies with the truth of God's Word.
   - Example: When faced with fear, declare, *"God hath not given us the spirit of fear; but of power, and of love, and of a sound mind"* (2 Timothy 1:7, KJV).

3. **Speak the Word**

    o   The words you speak reflect and reinforce your faith. Proverbs 18:21 teaches, *"Death and life are in the power of the tongue"* (KJV).

    o   Confess the promises of the cross over your life, such as, *"I am forgiven, redeemed, and victorious through Jesus Christ."*

    Wisdom Key: What you believe and speak aligns your life with the power of the cross.

The Eternal Perspective of Victory

1. **The Hope of Heaven**

    o   The cross guarantees eternal life for every believer. Revelation 21:4 promises, *"And God shall wipe away all tears from their eyes; and there shall be no more death, neither sorrow, nor crying, neither shall there be any more pain"* (KJV).

    o   This hope gives us strength to endure trials and live with purpose.

    Illustration: The story of Stephen, the first Christian martyr, demonstrates this hope. As he faced death, he saw the glory of God and declared, *"Lord Jesus, receive my spirit"* (Acts 7:59, KJV).

2. **Living with Confidence**

    - Because of the cross, we can face life with boldness, knowing that nothing can separate us from God's love (Romans 8:38-39, KJV).

    Action Step: Reflect on the eternal victory secured by Jesus, and let it shape your daily choices.

Closing Prayer

Heavenly Father,

Thank You for the victory of the cross and the freedom it brings to our lives. Help us to live each day in the power of Jesus' finished work, walking in freedom, peace, and purpose. Teach us to share this victory with others, that they too may experience the joy of salvation. Strengthen our faith and keep us anchored in the hope of eternity with You. In Jesus' name, we pray. Amen.

Wisdom Keys and Action Steps

- **Wisdom Keys:**
    - The cross was not the end of Jesus' story; it was the beginning of ours.
    - The victory of the cross is not just for eternity; it's for every moment of your life.
    - What you believe and speak aligns your life with the power of the cross.

- **Action Steps:**

  o Confess your sins and receive God's forgiveness daily.

  o Meditate on scriptures that declare your victory in Christ.

  o Speak God's promises over your life and circumstances.

Chapter 5:

"Take Up Your Cross":

The Cost of Commitment

"Take Up Your Cross": The Cost of Commitment

What Does It Mean to Take Up Your Cross?

Jesus Christ issued a profound call to His followers in Luke 9:23: *"If any man will come after me, let him deny himself, and take up his cross daily, and follow me"* (KJV). These words resonate as both a command and an invitation. They challenge believers to embrace the cost of true discipleship and surrender their lives wholly to God.

Taking up your cross does not mean bearing life's hardships without purpose. It symbolizes a deliberate and active commitment to the kingdom of God. It is an acknowledgment that the life Jesus calls us to live requires sacrifice, self-denial, and unwavering faith.

This chapter will unpack the meaning of taking up your cross, explore the cost of commitment, and provide practical insights into living out this vital command from Jesus. By the end, you will understand what it means to follow Christ fully and how to apply this powerful principle to your life.

Understanding the Cross of Commitment

1. **The Call to Deny Yourself**
    - Jesus' call to deny oneself is radical in a world driven by self-interest. He asks us to surrender our desires, ambitions, and plans to align with His will.

- Galatians 2:20 provides a key to understanding this: *"I am crucified with Christ: nevertheless I live; yet not I, but Christ liveth in me"* (KJV).

Illustration: Consider the rich young ruler in Mark 10:17-22. Though he had kept the commandments, he hesitated to sell his possessions and follow Jesus, revealing that his heart was still tied to earthly wealth. His unwillingness to deny himself cost him the joy of following Christ.

2. **The Cross as a Symbol of Sacrifice**

    - In Jesus' time, the cross was an instrument of death, symbolizing ultimate surrender. For believers, it represents laying down our lives—our rights, desires, and comforts—for the sake of Christ.

    - Romans 12:1 urges us, *"I beseech you therefore, brethren, by the mercies of God, that ye present your bodies a living sacrifice, holy, acceptable unto God, which is your reasonable service"* (KJV).

    Wisdom Key: Sacrifice is not losing something; it's gaining everything in Christ.

3. **The Daily Commitment**

    - Jesus emphasized taking up the cross *daily*. This is not a one-time decision but a continual commitment to live for God.

- Each day presents new opportunities to obey God, trust Him, and demonstrate His love to others.

Action Step: Begin each morning by dedicating your day to the Lord, asking for His strength to carry your cross faithfully.

The Cost of Commitment: Are You Willing to Pay the Price?

1. **The Cost of Obedience**

    - Obedience to God often requires letting go of what feels comfortable or safe. Abraham demonstrated this when he obeyed God's call to leave his homeland (Genesis 12:1-4). His willingness to obey paved the way for God's promises to be fulfilled.

    - Jesus Himself modeled perfect obedience, even unto death on the cross (Philippians 2:8).

    Illustration: The Apostle Paul faced shipwrecks, beatings, and imprisonment, yet he declared, *"I press toward the mark for the prize of the high calling of God in Christ Jesus"* (Philippians 3:14, KJV).

2. **The Cost of Rejection**

    - Following Christ often means standing against the world's values, which can lead to rejection or persecution.

- Jesus warned in John 15:18, *"If the world hate you, ye know that it hated me before it hated you"* (KJV).

Wisdom Key: Commitment to Christ may cost you the approval of others, but it secures the favor of God.

3. **The Cost of Prioritizing God's Kingdom**
   - Matthew 6:33 reminds us, *"But seek ye first the kingdom of God, and his righteousness; and all these things shall be added unto you"* (KJV). Prioritizing God's kingdom often requires reordering your time, resources, and relationships.
   - Illustration: Martha in Luke 10:38-42 was distracted by her duties, while Mary chose to sit at Jesus' feet. Jesus commended Mary for prioritizing what truly mattered.

Application: Living Out the Call to Take Up Your Cross

1. **Surrender Your Will to God**
   - Like Jesus in the Garden of Gethsemane, pray, *"Not my will, but thine, be done"* (Luke 22:42, KJV).
   - Surrender involves trusting God's plan even when it doesn't align with your preferences.

   Action Step: Write down one area of your life you need to surrender to God and pray for His guidance.

2. **Walk in Faith and Obedience**

   o   Faith fuels your ability to take up your cross. Hebrews 11 highlights heroes of faith who obeyed God despite the cost.

   o   Obedience demonstrates your trust in God's goodness and His promises.

   Wisdom Key: Faith and obedience go hand in hand; you cannot follow Christ without both.

3. **Embrace the Joy of the Cross**

   o   Though the cross represents sacrifice, it also leads to joy. Hebrews 12:2 declares, *"Looking unto Jesus the author and finisher of our faith; who for the joy that was set before him endured the cross"* (KJV).

   o   When you carry your cross, you share in Christ's suffering and His glory.

   Illustration: Missionaries who have given their lives for the Gospel often describe an unshakable joy in serving Christ, even in the face of hardship.

Practical Steps to Take Up Your Cross

1. **Examine Your Priorities**

   o   Are your choices and lifestyle centered on God's kingdom?

2. **Commit to Daily Prayer and Scripture Reading**
   - Spend time in God's presence to receive strength and direction.

3. **Serve Others Selflessly**
   - Taking up your cross involves loving others as Christ loved us.

4. **Stand Firm in the Face of Opposition**
   - Trust God to sustain you when you face rejection or persecution.

Action Step: Create a plan to incorporate these steps into your daily life, and ask someone you trust to hold you accountable.

The Reward of Commitment: Life Abundant and Eternal

1. **Abundant Life on Earth**
   - Jesus promised in John 10:10, *"I am come that they might have life, and that they might have it more abundantly"* (KJV).
   - Taking up your cross leads to a fulfilling and purposeful life.

2. **Eternal Life with Christ**
   - The ultimate reward of commitment is eternity with Jesus. Revelation 3:21 promises, *"To him that overcometh will I grant to sit with me in my throne"* (KJV).

Wisdom Key: The cost of commitment is temporary; the rewards are eternal.

Closing Prayer

Heavenly Father,

Thank You for the privilege of following Jesus. Help us to understand the depth of what it means to take up our cross and follow Him daily. Give us the strength to surrender our lives, trust in Your plan, and embrace the cost of commitment with joy. May we live lives that glorify You and reflect Your love to others. In Jesus' name, we pray. Amen.

Wisdom Keys and Action Steps

- **Wisdom Keys:**
    - Sacrifice is not losing something; it's gaining everything in Christ.
    - Faith and obedience go hand in hand; you cannot follow Christ without both.
    - The cost of commitment is temporary; the rewards are eternal.
- **Action Steps:**
    - Identify one area of your life where you need to deny yourself and submit to God.

- Make a daily habit of prayer and scripture reading to strengthen your faith.
- Look for ways to serve others sacrificially as an act of obedience to Christ.

Chapter 6:

"Peace Be Still":

Power Over Life's Storms

The Calm in Life's Chaos

Life is filled with storms. They come in many forms—illness, financial struggles, broken relationships, or emotional turmoil. In the midst of these challenges, we often feel overwhelmed, uncertain, and afraid. But Jesus, the Prince of Peace, has spoken three words that resonate across time and circumstances: *"Peace, be still"* (Mark 4:39, KJV).

These words reveal Christ's divine authority over the forces of nature, His deep concern for His followers, and His ability to bring peace into the storms of our lives. They remind us that no matter how chaotic our circumstances may be, God's peace is available to us when we trust in Him.

This chapter explores the profound power of Jesus' peace, how it transforms our lives, and how we can access it in every situation. By the end, you'll understand that casting your cares upon the Lord and trusting in His love allows you to find rest and reassurance even in life's fiercest storms.

Jesus' Peace in the Midst of the Storm

1. **The Storm on the Sea of Galilee**
    - In Mark 4:35-41, Jesus and His disciples were crossing the Sea of Galilee when a sudden storm arose. Waves crashed against their boat, threatening to sink it. The

disciples, terrified, cried out to Jesus, who was asleep in the stern.

- o Jesus arose, rebuked the wind, and spoke to the sea: *"Peace, be still." And the wind ceased, and there was a great calm* (Mark 4:39, KJV).

Illustration: This story isn't just about a physical storm; it's a metaphor for the trials we face in life. Like the disciples, we often focus on the size of the storm rather than the power of the One in our boat.

2. **The Nature of Jesus' Peace**

    - o Jesus' peace is not the absence of conflict or trouble but the presence of His assurance. In John 14:27, He promises: *"Peace I leave with you, my peace I give unto you: not as the world giveth, give I unto you"* (KJV).

    - o His peace is divine, unshaken by external circumstances, and rooted in His sovereignty and love.

Wisdom Key: True peace comes not from the absence of storms but from knowing the One who can calm them.

3. **Why We Struggle to Find Peace**

    - o Many believers struggle to find peace because they carry burdens they were never meant to bear. Jesus invites us in Matthew 11:28-30: *"Come unto me, all ye that labour and are heavy laden, and I will give you rest"* (KJV).

- When we hold onto our fears and anxieties instead of casting them upon the Lord, we rob ourselves of the peace He freely offers.

Theology of Peace: Faith, Trust, and Rest

1. **Faith Over Fear**

    - Jesus' question to the disciples, *"Why are ye so fearful? how is it that ye have no faith?"* (Mark 4:40, KJV), reveals that fear and faith cannot coexist. Faith in God's power and promises dispels fear.

    - Hebrews 11:6 reminds us, *"But without faith it is impossible to please him: for he that cometh to God must believe that he is"* (KJV).

    Illustration: When Peter walked on water in Matthew 14:22-33, he was fine as long as he kept his eyes on Jesus. But when he focused on the wind and waves, he began to sink. Faith keeps us afloat in life's storms.

2. **Trusting God's Sovereignty**

    - Trusting in God's sovereignty means believing that He is in control, even when we cannot see the outcome. Proverbs 3:5-6 urges us to *"Trust in the Lord with all thine heart; and lean not unto thine own understanding"* (KJV).

- Jesus' authority over the storm demonstrates His power over all creation and His ability to work all things together for good (Romans 8:28).

Wisdom Key: Trusting God means letting go of your need to control the outcome and resting in His care.

3. **Entering His Rest**

    - God's peace leads to rest—spiritual, emotional, and physical. Hebrews 4:9-10 speaks of a rest for the people of God, a rest that comes from ceasing our own works and relying on Him.

    Action Step: Identify one area of your life where you're striving instead of trusting. Surrender it to God in prayer and ask for His peace.

Application: Walking in the Peace of Christ

1. **Cast Your Cares Upon Him**

    - 1 Peter 5:7 instructs us to *"Casting all your care upon him; for he careth for you"* (KJV). This is not a passive act but a deliberate choice to entrust your worries to God.

    Action Step: Write down your top three concerns and pray over each one, releasing them to God.

2. **Meditate on His Promises**

    o The Word of God is a source of peace. Philippians 4:6-7 encourages us: *"Be careful for nothing; but in every thing by prayer and supplication with thanksgiving let your requests be made known unto God. And the peace of God, which passeth all understanding, shall keep your hearts and minds through Christ Jesus"* (KJV).

    Wisdom Key: When your mind is filled with God's promises, there is no room for fear or anxiety.

3. **Be Led by the Spirit**

    o The Holy Spirit is our Comforter, guiding us into all truth and filling us with peace (John 14:26-27).

    Illustration: Paul and Silas, imprisoned for preaching the Gospel, sang praises to God at midnight (Acts 16:25). Their peace was not dependent on their circumstances but on the presence of the Holy Spirit.

Practical Steps for Peace in Life's Storms

1. **Stay in the Word:** Read and meditate on scriptures that reinforce God's peace.
2. **Pray Continually:** Bring every concern to God in prayer.
3. **Worship Through the Storm:** Praise shifts your focus from the problem to the Problem Solver.

4. **Seek Fellowship:** Surround yourself with other believers who encourage your faith.

5. **Practice Gratitude:** Thank God for His blessings, even in difficult times.

Closing Prayer

Heavenly Father,

Thank You for the peace that surpasses all understanding. We come before You, casting our cares and burdens upon You, knowing that You care for us deeply. Help us to trust in Your sovereignty and rest in Your promises. Fill our hearts with faith and remind us daily that You are in control. May we walk in Your peace, glorifying You in every circumstance. In Jesus' name, Amen.

Wisdom Keys and Action Steps

- **Wisdom Keys:**
    - True peace comes not from the absence of storms but from knowing the One who can calm them.
    - Faith and fear cannot coexist; choose faith.
    - Trusting God means surrendering control and resting in His care.

- **Action Steps:**
    - Identify specific worries and surrender them to God in prayer.

- Memorize key scriptures on peace, such as Philippians 4:6-7 and John 14:27.
- Create a daily routine of prayer, worship, and scripture meditation to strengthen your trust in God.

Chapter 7:

"I Am the Light of the World": Walking in His Truth

The Power of Light in a World of Darkness

Darkness can be disorienting, isolating, and even terrifying. Imagine being lost in a vast wilderness at night, unable to see even a few feet ahead. A single beam of light piercing that darkness would immediately bring clarity, direction, and hope.

This is the reality of spiritual darkness—a life lived apart from God, where confusion and despair thrive. Into this darkness, Jesus spoke these powerful words: *"I am the light of the world: he that followeth me shall not walk in darkness, but shall have the light of life"* (John 8:12, KJV).

These words are not merely an invitation but a declaration of Jesus' divine role as the source of spiritual truth and life. In this chapter, we will explore what it means to walk in the light of His Word, shine brightly for Him in a dark world, and receive His light into our spirit.

Understanding Jesus as the Light of the World

1. **The Symbolism of Light in Scripture**

    Throughout the Bible, light is a consistent symbol of God's presence, truth, and holiness. In Genesis 1:3, God's first act in creation was to command, *"Let there be light."* This light was not merely physical; it represented order triumphing over chaos.

Theological Insight: Jesus fulfills this symbolism. In John 1:4-5, we are told, *"In him was life; and the life was the light of men. And the light shineth in darkness; and the darkness comprehended it not"* (KJV). Jesus is the eternal Light that dispels the chaos of sin and death.

2. **The Context of Jesus' Declaration**

    Jesus made His bold declaration during the Feast of Tabernacles, a time when massive lamps lit the temple courtyards in celebration of God's guidance as a pillar of fire in the wilderness. Standing amidst these lights, Jesus proclaimed Himself to be the true and eternal Light.

    Illustration: Just as the pillar of fire led the Israelites through the wilderness, Jesus leads us through the challenges of life. Without Him, we are left to wander aimlessly in spiritual darkness.

3. **The Light That Exposes and Guides**

    Light serves two critical purposes: it exposes what is hidden and provides a path forward. Hebrews 4:12 says, *"For the word of God is quick, and powerful, and sharper than any twoedged sword… and is a discerner of the thoughts and intents of the heart"* (KJV). Jesus, as the living Word, exposes the truth about our condition and guides us toward righteousness.

Practical Application: Walking in His Light

1. **Receiving the Light of the World**

   The first step to walking in the light is to receive Jesus as Lord and Savior. In John 12:46, Jesus says, *"I am come a light into the world, that whosoever believeth on me should not abide in darkness"* (KJV).

   Action Step: Reflect on areas of your life where spiritual darkness—sin, confusion, or fear—may still linger. Surrender these areas to God in prayer, asking Him to illuminate them with His truth.

2. **Walking Daily in His Light**

   Walking in the light requires daily communion with God through prayer and Scripture. Psalm 119:105 reminds us, *"Thy word is a lamp unto my feet, and a light unto my path"* (KJV).

   Illustration: A lighthouse guides sailors safely to shore, warning them of hidden dangers. Similarly, God's Word guides us, revealing the hazards of sin and the path to righteousness.

   Wisdom Key: Consistency is key. A flashlight that isn't charged won't provide light when you need it. Stay charged by remaining in constant fellowship with God.

3. **Reflecting His Light to Others**

   As followers of Christ, we are called to reflect His light. Matthew 5:16 says, *"Let your light so shine before men, that they may see your good works, and glorify your Father which is in heaven"* (KJV).

   Illustration: The moon has no light of its own; it reflects the light of the sun. In the same way, our lives should reflect the light of Christ, drawing others to Him.

Theology of Light: Faith, Hope, and Love

1. **Faith to Walk in the Light**

   Walking in the light begins with faith. Hebrews 11:6 declares, *"Without faith it is impossible to please him"* (KJV). Faith allows us to trust God's guidance even when the path ahead seems unclear.

2. **Hope Anchored in the Light**

   Hope sustains us in the face of life's challenges. Romans 15:13 reminds us, *"Now the God of hope fill you with all joy and peace in believing, that ye may abound in hope, through the power of the Holy Ghost"* (KJV).

3. **Love as the Expression of the Light**

   Love is the practical outworking of walking in the light. 1 John 2:10 says, *"He that loveth his brother abideth in the light, and there is none occasion of stumbling in him"* (KJV).

Wisdom Keys and Action Steps

- **Wisdom Keys:**
  - The light of Christ brings clarity and peace.
  - To walk in the light, we must stay rooted in the Word.
  - Reflecting Christ's light draws others to Him.
- **Action Steps:**
  - Spend 15 minutes daily reading and meditating on Scripture.
  - Identify one way you can reflect Christ's light to someone this week, whether through an act of kindness, encouragement, or sharing the gospel.
  - Memorize John 8:12 and use it as a declaration of faith in times of spiritual darkness.

Illustrations from Scripture

1. **The Light That Transformed Paul**

   On the road to Damascus, Paul was engulfed in a literal and spiritual light that changed the trajectory of his life (Acts 9:3-6). This encounter reminds us of the transformative power of Christ's light.

2. **The Lamp of Gideon's Victory**

   Gideon's small army defeated the Midianites by breaking clay jars to reveal hidden torches (Judges 7:16-22). This act symbolizes how God's light within us can bring victory over seemingly insurmountable challenges.

Closing Prayer

Heavenly Father,

Thank You for sending Jesus, the Light of the World, to guide us out of darkness and into Your truth. Help us to receive His light into our hearts, to walk faithfully in His Word, and to shine brightly in a world desperately in need of hope. Empower us to reflect His love and truth in all we do, so that others may see Your glory and be drawn to You. In Jesus' name, Amen.

Chapter 8:

"Let Not Your Heart Be Troubled": Hope for Troubled Times

The Battleground of the Heart

In John 14:1, Jesus speaks words of comfort and command: *"Let not your heart be troubled: ye believe in God, believe also in me"* (KJV). These words were spoken to His disciples during a time of uncertainty and impending sorrow. But they are just as relevant to us today.

The heart, in Scripture, represents the core of our being—our emotions, will, and thoughts. However, Jeremiah 17:9 reminds us, *"The heart is deceitful above all things, and desperately wicked: who can know it?"* (KJV). Because of its tendency to deceive, we are warned not to lean on our own understanding or trust in our heart's instincts. Instead, Jesus invites us to trust wholly in Him, allowing His Word to guard and guide us.

In this chapter, we will explore what it means to guard our hearts with God's Word, follow Him in obedience, and trust in His unfailing provision. We'll uncover the practical steps necessary to overcome life's troubles with the assurance of His hope.

The Deceitful Nature of the Heart

1. **Why We Should Not Trust in Our Hearts**

    The Bible consistently warns us about the unreliable nature of the human heart. It is swayed by emotions, circumstances, and desires that often conflict with God's truth. Proverbs

3:5 teaches, *"Trust in the Lord with all thine heart; and lean not unto thine own understanding"* (KJV).

Theological Insight: Our hearts, when left unchecked, can lead us away from God's will. This is why Jesus emphasizes the importance of believing in Him and His words. Trusting in God's truth transforms our hearts and aligns them with His purposes.

2. **Guarding the Heart Through Scripture**

Psalm 119:11 says, *"Thy word have I hid in mine heart, that I might not sin against thee"* (KJV). The Word of God is the safeguard that protects us from deception. By filling our hearts with His truth, we establish a firm foundation that withstands the storms of life.

Illustrations from Scripture: Trusting in God Over the Heart

1. **Peter Walking on Water (Matthew 14:28-31)**

When Peter stepped out of the boat to walk on water, his faith was initially anchored in Jesus' command. But as he focused on the wind and waves, fear crept into his heart, and he began to sink.

Lesson: Peter's experience reminds us that when we trust in circumstances or our own emotions, we falter. But when we keep our eyes on Jesus, we find stability and strength.

2. **David's Trust in God Over His Own Heart (1 Samuel 30:6)**

   After the Amalekites raided Ziklag, David's men spoke of stoning him in their despair. Yet, David *"encouraged himself in the Lord his God"* (KJV). Instead of succumbing to fear, David sought God's guidance and found victory.

   Lesson: David chose to trust God's provision rather than react out of his emotions. This is the essence of guarding our hearts with His Word.

Application: Steps to Guard Your Heart

1. **Anchor Yourself in God's Word**

   The Word of God is a light that dispels darkness and a shield that deflects doubt. When we fill our hearts with Scripture, we create a spiritual defense against the lies of the enemy.

   Action Step: Commit to daily Bible reading and memorization. Start with verses like Philippians 4:6-7 and Isaiah 26:3, which emphasize God's peace and trustworthiness.

2. **Pray and Surrender Daily**

   Prayer aligns our hearts with God's will. Philippians 4:6 encourages us to *"be careful for nothing; but in every thing by prayer and supplication with thanksgiving let your requests be made known unto God"* (KJV).

Illustration: Jesus Himself modeled this in the Garden of Gethsemane, praying, *"Not my will, but thine, be done"* (Luke 22:42, KJV). When we surrender our desires to God, we find peace and direction.

3. **Rely on the Holy Spirit**

   The Holy Spirit is our comforter and guide. He empowers us to discern truth and reject the deceitfulness of our own hearts.

   Action Step: Begin each day by asking the Holy Spirit to guide your thoughts and actions. Trust in His leading rather than your own understanding.

Biblical Examples of Trust and Obedience

1. **Abraham's Faith in God's Provision (Genesis 22:1-14)**

   When God asked Abraham to sacrifice Isaac, his beloved son, Abraham obeyed without hesitation. His heart was anchored in trust, not emotion.

   Application: Abraham's story teaches us to trust in God's provision, even when His commands seem difficult or unclear.

2. **The Widow of Zarephath (1 Kings 17:8-16)**

   Despite her dire circumstances, the widow obeyed Elijah's request for food, trusting in God's promise of provision. Her obedience brought miraculous supply.

   Application: Trusting God often requires taking steps of faith, even when we don't fully understand His plan.

Wisdom Keys and Practical Insights

- **Wisdom Keys:**
  - Trusting in your heart leads to confusion; trusting in God leads to peace.
  - Scripture is the anchor that keeps your heart steadfast.
  - Surrendering to God's will brings clarity and direction.

- **Practical Steps:**
  - **Daily Devotion:** Spend time each day in Scripture and prayer.
  - **Guard Your Influences:** Be mindful of what you allow into your heart through media, relationships, and thoughts.
  - **Seek Godly Counsel:** Surround yourself with believers who encourage and challenge you in your faith.

Reflection: Trusting God in Troubled Times

Take a moment to reflect on areas where you may be relying on your own heart or understanding. What steps can you take today to shift your trust to God? How can you guard your heart more diligently against fear, doubt, and deception?

Closing Prayer

Heavenly Father,

Thank You for Your Word, which guards and guides our hearts. Teach us to trust in You rather than in our own understanding. Help us to surrender our fears and anxieties to You, knowing that You are faithful to provide. Fill our hearts with Your peace and anchor us in Your truth. Holy Spirit, lead us daily as we seek to follow Your will. In Jesus' name, Amen.

This chapter equips us to navigate troubled times with hope, anchored in the unchanging promises of God. By guarding our hearts and trusting in His provision, we can walk confidently, knowing that He is with us every step of the way.

Chapter 9:

"Come Unto Me": Finding Rest in Jesus

The Invitation of a Lifetime

In Matthew 11:28-30, Jesus extends one of the most profound invitations ever spoken: *"Come unto me, all ye that labour and are heavy laden, and I will give you rest. Take my yoke upon you, and learn of me; for I am meek and lowly in heart: and ye shall find rest unto your souls. For my yoke is easy, and my burden is light"* (KJV).

These words are not just comforting—they are transformative. They reveal the heart of a Savior who desires to bear our burdens and give us peace. Yet, there is a condition attached: *we must come to Him.* The rest He promises is not automatic; it requires action on our part.

This chapter explores what it means to come to Jesus, why it is our responsibility to do so, and how His promised rest transforms every aspect of our lives. Through scriptural exposition, practical application, and spiritual insight, we'll discover the key to experiencing the rest Jesus offers.

The Power of the Invitation

1. **A Call to All Who Labor and Are Heavy Laden**

    Jesus speaks to the weary and burdened—those carrying the weight of sin, worry, and the struggles of life. His invitation is universal, yet deeply personal. It is a call to lay down our efforts and trust in Him.

- **Theological Insight:** The burden of sin is one we cannot bear alone. Romans 3:23 reminds us, *"For all have sinned, and come short of the glory of God"* (KJV). Jesus' call to "come" is an invitation to exchange our inadequacy for His sufficiency.

2. **The Rest He Promises**

   The rest Jesus offers is not merely physical but spiritual. It is the peace that comes from being reconciled to God and the assurance of His provision in our lives.

   - **Illustration:** Consider the story of the prodigal son (Luke 15:11-32). When the son returned to his father, he found rest—not in his own strength, but in the father's embrace. His journey home mirrors our need to come to Jesus to find true peace.

The Responsibility to Come

1. **Why We Must Take the First Step**

   God has given us free will, and He will not force us to come to Him. Revelation 3:20 says, *"Behold, I stand at the door, and knock: if any man hear my voice, and open the door, I will come in to him, and will sup with him, and he with me"* (KJV).

   - **Illustration:** In the healing of the woman with the issue of blood (Mark 5:25-34), Jesus did not go to her—she came to Him, pressing through the crowd in faith. Her determination and action brought her healing.

2. **Obedience Unlocks the Promise** Coming to Jesus requires humility and obedience. James 4:8 tells us, *"Draw nigh to God, and he will draw nigh to you"* (KJV). When we take the step of faith to approach Him, we open the door to His blessings.

   o **Theological Insight:** Rest is the fruit of faith. Hebrews 4:11 exhorts us, *"Let us labour therefore to enter into that rest, lest any man fall after the same example of unbelief"* (KJV). Coming to Jesus involves active faith—a willingness to trust Him fully.

Illustrations from Scripture: Coming to Jesus

1. **Bartimaeus the Blind Beggar (Mark 10:46-52)**

   Bartimaeus cried out to Jesus, refusing to let the crowd silence him. When Jesus called him forward, Bartimaeus came without hesitation and received his sight.

   o **Lesson:** Bartimaeus' story shows us the urgency and determination required to come to Jesus. We must not let distractions or doubts keep us from responding to His call.

2. **The Samaritan Woman at the Well (John 4:7-26)**

   Jesus met the Samaritan woman in her brokenness, offering her living water. Her willingness to engage with Him led to her transformation and testimony.

- **Lesson:** Coming to Jesus often means confronting uncomfortable truths about ourselves, but the result is life-changing grace and freedom.

Application: Steps to Come to Jesus

1. **Acknowledge Your Need**

   The first step in coming to Jesus is recognizing your need for Him. Whether it's the burden of sin, fear, or weariness, we must admit that we cannot find rest apart from Him.

   Action Step: Take time to reflect on the areas of your life where you need Jesus' intervention. Write them down as a prayer of surrender.

2. **Respond to His Invitation**

   Jesus is always calling us to Himself, but we must respond. This requires humility, faith, and a willingness to let go of our burdens.

   Action Step: Spend time in prayer, verbally committing your heart and life to Jesus.

3. **Learn of Him**

   Jesus says, *"Take my yoke upon you, and learn of me"* (Matthew 11:29, KJV). Coming to Jesus is not a one-time event but a lifelong journey of discipleship.

Action Step: Dedicate time each day to studying His Word and growing in your understanding of His character and promises.

Wisdom Keys and Practical Insights

- **Wisdom Keys:**
  - Rest is found not in striving but in surrender.
  - Jesus' invitation requires a response—He will not force His rest upon us.
  - Learning from Jesus brings peace and purpose to our lives.
- **Practical Steps:**
  - **Daily Devotion:** Set aside time each morning to pray and read Scripture.
  - **Cast Your Burdens:** Write down your worries and pray over them, asking Jesus to take them from you.
  - **Join a Community:** Surround yourself with believers who encourage you to grow in your faith.

Reflection: Are You Coming to Jesus?

Take a moment to evaluate your heart. Are there areas where you are holding back from coming to Jesus? What steps can you take today to draw closer to Him and experience His rest?

Closing Prayer

Lord Jesus,

Thank You for the invitation to come to You and find rest. I acknowledge my need for Your grace and peace. Help me to respond to Your call with faith and humility, laying down my burdens and trusting in Your provision. Teach me to walk with You daily, learning from Your example and relying on Your strength. Fill my heart with the rest that only You can provide. In Your precious name, Amen.

In coming to Jesus, we find the rest our souls desperately need. It is not a passive act but an active choice to trust in His promises and follow His leading. When we come to Him, we experience the peace and joy that only He can provide.

Chapter 10:

"I Am the Resurrection and the Life": The Promise of Eternity

"I Am the Resurrection and the Life": The Promise of Eternity

The Hope Beyond the Grave

In John 11:25-26, Jesus proclaimed: *"I am the resurrection, and the life: he that believeth in me, though he were dead, yet shall he live: And whosoever liveth and believeth in me shall never die"* (KJV). These words, spoken at the tomb of Lazarus, hold the key to understanding the believer's eternal hope. Jesus is not just the giver of life; He is life itself.

This chapter will delve into the promise of eternity that Jesus offers to those who believe in Him. We will explore the heavenly home He has prepared, the glorious reality of the rapture, and the transformation that awaits all who have trusted in Him. Through the lens of Scripture, we will understand the eternal victory secured by His resurrection and how this hope transforms our present lives.

1: Jesus, the Resurrection and the Life

1. **The Context of the Claim**

    In John 11, Jesus arrives in Bethany after Lazarus has been in the grave for four days. Martha meets Him with a mixture of grief and faith, saying, *"Lord, if thou hadst been here, my brother had not died"* (John 11:21, KJV). Jesus responds with a declaration that shifts the narrative from death to life: *"I am the resurrection, and the life"* (John 11:25, KJV).

    - **Theological Insight:** This statement underscores Jesus' power over death and His role as the source of eternal life. Death is not the end for those who believe in Him; it is a transition into everlasting life.

2. **Illustration: Lazarus Raised from the Dead**

   Jesus' authority over death is demonstrated when He commands Lazarus to come forth. This miraculous act serves as a foretaste of the resurrection that awaits all believers.

   - **Lesson:** Just as Lazarus responded to Jesus' call, we too must respond to His invitation to experience eternal life.

2: The Promise of a Heavenly Home

1. **Jesus' Assurance in John 14**

   On the eve of His crucifixion, Jesus comforts His disciples with these words: *"Let not your heart be troubled: ye believe in God, believe also in me. In my Father's house are many mansions: if it were not so, I would have told you. I go to prepare a place for you"* (John 14:1-2, KJV).

   - **Theological Insight:** Jesus' promise of a heavenly home assures us that eternity is not a vague concept but a prepared place for those who trust in Him.

2. **A Glimpse of Heaven**

   The apostle John provides a vivid description of heaven in Revelation 21: *"And I saw a new heaven and a new earth: for the first heaven and the first earth were passed away"* (Revelation 21:1,

KJV). He speaks of streets of gold, gates of pearl, and the absence of sorrow and pain.

- **Illustration:** The vision of heaven reminds us of the eternal joy that awaits believers. It is a place of perfect peace, where God Himself will dwell with His people.

3: The Glorious Reality of the Rapture

1. **The Pre-Tribulation View of the Rapture**

   According to 1 Thessalonians 4:16-17, *"For the Lord himself shall descend from heaven with a shout, with the voice of the archangel, and with the trump of God: and the dead in Christ shall rise first: Then we which are alive and remain shall be caught up together with them in the clouds, to meet the Lord in the air"* (KJV).

   - **Theological Insight:** The rapture is the moment when Christ will gather His church, sparing believers from the tribulation period described in Revelation. This pre-tribulation view emphasizes God's faithfulness to deliver His people from wrath.

2. **The Transformation of the Saints**

   Paul writes in 1 Corinthians 15:51-52, *"We shall not all sleep, but we shall all be changed, In a moment, in the twinkling of an eye, at the last trump"* (KJV). Both the living and the dead in Christ will receive glorified bodies, free from sin and decay.

   - **Illustration:** Imagine the joy of reunion when loved ones who have gone before are raised in glory. The rapture is not just a theological concept—it is the fulfillment of God's promise to His children.

4: Living in Light of Eternity

1. **Suffering Prepares Us for Glory**

   Romans 8:18 reminds us, *"For I reckon that the sufferings of this present time are not worthy to be compared with the glory which shall be revealed in us"* (KJV). Our trials are temporary, but the reward is eternal.

   - **Illustration:** Consider the apostles who endured persecution yet rejoiced in the hope of eternal life. Their faith inspires us to persevere, knowing that our labor is not in vain.

2. **Obedience and Trust**

   To inherit the promise of eternity, we must walk in obedience to Christ. Hebrews 11 showcases heroes of faith who trusted God's promises, even when they could not see the outcome.

5: Wisdom Keys and Practical Application

- **Wisdom Keys:**
  - Jesus' resurrection is the cornerstone of our faith and hope.
  - Heaven is a prepared place for a prepared people.

- The rapture offers hope and urgency to live for Christ today.
- **Practical Steps:**
  - **Anchor Your Faith:** Study Scriptures about heaven and the resurrection to strengthen your hope.
  - **Share the Gospel:** The promise of eternity compels us to share Christ with others.
  - **Live with Purpose:** Let the reality of eternity shape your priorities and decisions.

Closing Reflection and Prayer

As we consider Jesus' promise of eternity, let us examine our hearts. Are we living in the hope of His return? Are we sharing the good news of eternal life with those around us?

Prayer:

Heavenly Father,

Thank You for the promise of eternal life through Jesus Christ. Help us to live in the light of this hope, trusting in Your Word and sharing Your love with others. Strengthen our faith as we await the glorious day when we will see You face to face. May we remain steadfast in obedience and joyful in the assurance of Your promises. In Jesus' name, Amen.

The promise of eternity transforms not only our future but our present. By trusting in Jesus as the resurrection and the life, we can face each day with confidence, knowing that our hope is secure in Him.

Chapter II:
"Go Ye Therefore":
The Great Commission

The Call to Go

The last words of Jesus to His disciples before His ascension were not merely a farewell; they were a command—a commission that would define their mission and, by extension, ours. In Matthew 28:18-20, Jesus declared:

"All power is given unto me in heaven and in earth. Go ye therefore, and teach all nations, baptizing them in the name of the Father, and of the Son, and of the Holy Ghost: Teaching them to observe all things whatsoever I have commanded you: and, lo, I am with you alway, even unto the end of the world. Amen" (KJV).

The Great Commission is not optional. It is a divine mandate to every believer. Jesus sends us into the world with the authority of heaven and the promise of His presence. This chapter explores the depth of this commission, the role of the Holy Spirit in guiding us, and the relationship between faith, works, and salvation.

By the end, you will understand how to live out this call and how to faithfully represent Christ as His workman, rightly dividing the Word of truth.

1: Commissioned to Go

1. **Understanding the Authority of Jesus**

    Jesus begins the Great Commission by affirming His authority: *"All power is given unto me in heaven and in earth"* (Matthew 28:18, KJV). This power is the foundation for our mission. He does not send us in our strength but in His.

- **Illustration:** Imagine a soldier sent into battle without proper authority or resources. Such a mission would be futile. But when sent by the highest authority, with full provision, the soldier moves with confidence. Similarly, we go into the world under the authority of the King of kings.

2. **The Call to All Nations**

   The command to "teach all nations" emphasizes the global nature of the gospel. The message of salvation is not confined to one people group or culture; it is for every tribe, tongue, and nation.

   - **Biblical Example:** In Acts 10, Peter's vision and his visit to Cornelius, a Gentile, illustrate the breaking of cultural barriers. The Holy Spirit confirmed that the gospel was for all, showing no partiality.

2: Guided by the Holy Spirit

1. **The Role of the Holy Spirit**

   Jesus assured His disciples: *"But ye shall receive power, after that the Holy Ghost is come upon you: and ye shall be witnesses unto me both in Jerusalem, and in all Judaea, and in Samaria, and unto the uttermost part of the earth"* (Acts 1:8, KJV).

   - **Theological Insight:** The Holy Spirit empowers and guides us in fulfilling the Great Commission. Without His leading, our efforts are fruitless.

2. **Illustration: Philip and the Ethiopian Eunuch**

   In Acts 8:26-40, Philip was directed by the Spirit to meet the Ethiopian eunuch. Philip's obedience led to the eunuch understanding Isaiah's prophecy and receiving Jesus as his Savior.

   - **Lesson:** When we are sensitive to the Holy Spirit, He opens doors for us to share the gospel and leads us to those who are ready to hear it.

3: Salvation by Faith, Not Works

1. **The Truth of Salvation**

   Ephesians 2:8-9 declares: *"For by grace are ye saved through faith; and that not of yourselves: it is the gift of God: Not of works, lest any man should boast"* (KJV). Salvation is a gift, not a reward for good behavior.

   - **Illustration:** The thief on the cross (Luke 23:39-43) had no opportunity to perform good works, yet Jesus assured him of paradise because of his faith.

2. **Works as a Byproduct of Love**

   While works do not save us, they are evidence of our faith. James 2:26 reminds us: *"For as the body without the spirit is dead, so faith without works is dead also"* (KJV). True faith produces action.

- o **Theological Insight:** Works flow naturally when we love God. They are not a means to earn salvation but a response to the grace we have received.

4: Studying to Show Ourselves Approved

1. **The Importance of Scripture**

   2 Timothy 2:15 urges us: *"Study to shew thyself approved unto God, a workman that needeth not to be ashamed, rightly dividing the word of truth"* (KJV). To effectively share the gospel, we must be grounded in the Word.

   - o **Practical Step:** Develop a habit of daily Bible study. Begin with passages that emphasize the gospel message, such as John 3, Romans 5, and Ephesians 2.

2. **Equipped for Every Good Work**

   2 Timothy 3:16-17 states: *"All scripture is given by inspiration of God, and is profitable for doctrine, for reproof, for correction, for instruction in righteousness: That the man of God may be perfect, throughly furnished unto all good works"* (KJV). The Word equips us for the mission.

5: Wisdom Keys and Practical Application

- **Wisdom Keys:**
  - o Jesus sends us with His authority and presence.
  - o Salvation is a gift, but works are the fruit of faith.

- o The Holy Spirit is our guide and empowers our witness.
- **Practical Steps:**
  - o **Pray for Boldness:** Ask God to give you the courage to share the gospel.
  - o **Listen to the Holy Spirit:** Be sensitive to His leading in everyday interactions.
  - o **Equip Yourself:** Study Scripture to deepen your understanding and confidence.
  - o **Build Relationships:** Evangelism often begins with genuine connections.

Closing Reflection and Prayer

The Great Commission is not a task reserved for a select few. It is the calling of every believer. Jesus has equipped us with His authority, empowered us with His Spirit, and entrusted us with His message. As we go, let us remember that He is with us always, guiding and strengthening us.

Prayer:

Heavenly Father,

Thank You for the privilege of being Your witnesses in this world. Help us to walk in obedience to the Great Commission, relying on Your authority and the guidance of the Holy Spirit. Give us boldness to share the good news and compassion for the lost.

May our lives reflect the love and truth of Jesus Christ, drawing others to Your kingdom. In Jesus' name, Amen.

The Great Commission is not just a call to action—it is a way of life. As we study, serve, and share, may we fulfill our role as Christ's ambassadors, bringing the hope of salvation to a world in need

Chapter 12:

"Lo, I Am with You Always": The Promise of His Presence

The Comfort of His Presence

Among the most powerful assurances Jesus gave His disciples are found in Matthew 28:20: *"And, lo, I am with you always, even unto the end of the world. Amen"* (KJV). These words are more than a comforting thought; they are a life-transforming truth. Jesus' promise of His eternal presence is the anchor for every believer's life.

This chapter explores how Jesus fulfills this promise through the sending of the Holy Spirit, our Helper, Teacher, and Comforter. We will uncover the benefits of living with the indwelling Spirit and provide practical steps to receive and walk in His presence daily.

By the end of this chapter, you will understand how to embrace the presence of God, rely on His Spirit, and experience the abundant life promised to every believer.

1: Jesus' Promise to Never Leave Us

1. **The Eternal Presence of Christ**

    Jesus' words in Matthew 28:20 were spoken to His disciples as part of the Great Commission. However, the promise is timeless and applies to all who follow Him.

    - **Scriptural Assurance:** In Hebrews 13:5, we are reminded: *"I will never leave thee, nor forsake thee"* (KJV). This declaration of God's faithfulness brings peace in times of trouble and strength in times of weakness.

- **Illustration:** Consider the story of Joseph in Genesis. Though betrayed, enslaved, and imprisoned, Scripture repeatedly states: *"The Lord was with Joseph"* (Genesis 39:2, 21, KJV). God's presence sustained him through every trial and elevated him to fulfill His divine purpose.

2: The Holy Spirit: The Fulfillment of the Promise

1. **Jesus' Prayer for the Comforter**

   Before His crucifixion, Jesus assured His disciples of the coming of the Holy Spirit: *"And I will pray the Father, and he shall give you another Comforter, that he may abide with you forever"* (John 14:16, KJV).

   - **Role of the Holy Spirit:** The Holy Spirit is our Helper, Teacher, and Comforter. He is the manifest presence of God in our lives, equipping us for every good work and leading us into all truth (John 14:26).

2. **Pentecost: The Arrival of the Holy Spirit**

   In Acts 2, the promise was fulfilled. The Holy Spirit descended upon the believers, empowering them to be witnesses and transforming them into bold ambassadors for Christ.

   - **Theological Insight:** The indwelling Holy Spirit is a seal of our salvation (Ephesians 1:13-14) and the source of our strength, wisdom, and comfort.

3: The Benefits of His Presence

1. **Peace Beyond Understanding**

    o **Scripture:** Philippians 4:7 promises: *"And the peace of God, which passeth all understanding, shall keep your hearts and minds through Christ Jesus"* (KJV).

    o **Illustration:** In Mark 4:35-41, Jesus calmed the storm with the words, *"Peace, be still"* (KJV). His presence brought peace to the disciples' fearful hearts, demonstrating that no storm is greater than His authority.

2. **Guidance in All Truth**

    o **Scripture:** *"Howbeit when he, the Spirit of truth, is come, he will guide you into all truth"* (John 16:13, KJV).

    o **Practical Application:** The Holy Spirit reveals the will of God through Scripture and prayer. By yielding to His guidance, we make wise decisions and align ourselves with God's purpose.

3. **Empowerment for Witnessing**

    o **Scripture:** Acts 1:8 declares: *"But ye shall receive power, after that the Holy Ghost is come upon you: and ye shall be witnesses unto me"* (KJV).

- **Illustration:** Peter, once fearful and denying Christ, boldly preached at Pentecost after being filled with the Spirit, leading 3,000 souls to salvation (Acts 2:41).

4: How to Receive the Promise of the Holy Spirit

1. **Step 1: Believe in Jesus Christ**

    - **Scripture:** *"He that believeth on me, as the scripture hath said, out of his belly shall flow rivers of living water"* (John 7:38, KJV).

    - **Application:** Salvation is the prerequisite for receiving the Holy Spirit. Acknowledge Jesus as Lord and Savior and believe in His finished work on the cross.

2. **Step 2: Ask for the Holy Spirit**

    - **Scripture:** *"If ye then, being evil, know how to give good gifts unto your children: how much more shall your heavenly Father give the Holy Spirit to them that ask him?"* (Luke 11:13, KJV).

    - **Action Step:** In prayer, ask God to fill you with His Spirit. Approach Him with faith, believing His promise.

3. **Step 3: Yield to His Leading**

    - **Scripture:** *"Walk in the Spirit, and ye shall not fulfil the lust of the flesh"* (Galatians 5:16, KJV).

    - **Application:** Surrender your will to God daily. Allow the Spirit to guide your decisions, words, and actions.

4. **Step 4: Abide in the Word**

    - **Scripture:** *"If ye abide in me, and my words abide in you, ye shall ask what ye will, and it shall be done unto you"* (John 15:7, KJV).

    - **Action Step:** Regularly study and meditate on Scripture. The Word of God is the Spirit's primary tool for transforming your mind and heart.

5: Wisdom Keys and Practical Application

- **Wisdom Keys:**

    - The presence of Jesus is a constant promise for every believer.

    - The Holy Spirit equips, comforts, and empowers us for victorious living.

    - Faith and surrender are the keys to experiencing His presence fully.

- **Practical Steps:**

    - Develop a habit of daily prayer and Scripture reading.

    - Practice listening to the voice of the Holy Spirit in quiet moments.

    - Trust God's presence in trials, knowing He is with you always.

Closing Reflection and Prayer

As believers, we are never alone. Jesus' promise to be with us always is fulfilled through the indwelling Holy Spirit. This divine presence gives us peace, guidance, and power for every aspect of life.

Prayer:

Heavenly Father,

Thank You for the promise of Your presence. Thank You for sending the Holy Spirit to guide, teach, and comfort us. Help us to walk daily in the awareness of Your presence and to yield our hearts and minds to the Spirit's leading. Strengthen us to live victoriously and boldly proclaim Your name to the world. In Jesus' name, Amen.

Let this truth transform your life: You are never alone. His presence is your strength, your guide, and your peace. Rest in His promise, and walk confidently in the assurance that He is with you always.

Chapter 13:

"Thy Sins Be Forgiven Thee": The Power of Mercy

The Greatest Need of Humanity

One of the most profound statements Jesus ever made is found in Matthew 9:2: *"Son, be of good cheer; thy sins be forgiven thee."* These words reveal the heart of the gospel—the message of mercy, forgiveness, and freedom. Humanity's greatest need is not wealth, health, or success; it is forgiveness. Sin separates us from God, but through Jesus, we are reconciled to Him.

This chapter unpacks the power of mercy and the significance of Jesus' death, burial, and resurrection. By the end, you will understand how to receive forgiveness, live free from condemnation, and walk confidently as a child of God.

1: The Problem of Sin and the Price of Redemption

1. **What is Sin?**

    - Sin is any action, thought, or attitude that goes against God's holiness. Romans 3:23 states, *"For all have sinned, and come short of the glory of God."* Sin separates us from God and brings spiritual death (Romans 6:23).

    - **Illustration:** In the Garden of Eden, Adam and Eve's disobedience introduced sin into the world (Genesis 3). Their sin not only led to separation from God but also brought suffering, death, and condemnation to all humanity.

2. **The Price of Redemption**

    - God's holiness demands justice, but His love provides mercy. Jesus paid the ultimate price for our sin through

His death on the cross. Isaiah 53:5 declares: *"But he was wounded for our transgressions, he was bruised for our iniquities: the chastisement of our peace was upon him; and with his stripes we are healed."*

- **Theological Insight:** Jesus became the perfect sacrifice, fulfilling the requirements of the law (Hebrews 10:10). His blood cleanses us from all sin (1 John 1:7).

2: The Power of the Cross and Resurrection

1. **Jesus' Death on the Cross**

   At Calvary, Jesus willingly laid down His life. His final words, *"It is finished"* (John 19:30), declared that the debt of sin was paid in full. The cross was not a defeat but a victory over sin, death, and the devil.

   - **Illustration:** In Luke 23:39-43, Jesus forgave the repentant thief on the cross, saying, *"Verily I say unto thee, Today shalt thou be with me in paradise."* This moment demonstrates the immediate and complete forgiveness available to all who believe.

2. **The Power of the Resurrection**

   The resurrection is proof that Jesus defeated death and secured eternal life for believers. Paul writes in 1 Corinthians 15:17: *"And if Christ be not raised, your faith is vain; ye are yet in your sins."* The empty tomb is our assurance that sin's penalty is paid, and we are justified before God (Romans 4:25).

3: Living Free from Condemnation

1. **Freedom in Christ**

    Romans 8:1 promises: *"There is therefore now no condemnation to them which are in Christ Jesus, who walk not after the flesh, but after the Spirit."* Through faith in Jesus, we are forgiven and free from the guilt of our past.

    - **Application:** Stop carrying the burden of sins that Jesus has already forgiven. When the enemy tries to remind you of your past, remind him of the cross.

2. **A New Identity**

    2 Corinthians 5:17 declares: *"Therefore if any man be in Christ, he is a new creature: old things are passed away; behold, all things are become new."* In Christ, we are no longer slaves to sin but children of God.

    - **Wisdom Key:** Your past does not define you; your identity in Christ does.

4: How to Receive Forgiveness

1. **Believe in the Finished Work of Christ**

    - **Scripture:** *"That if thou shalt confess with thy mouth the Lord Jesus, and shalt believe in thine heart that God hath raised him from the dead, thou shalt be saved"* (Romans 10:9).

    - **Action Step:** Acknowledge your need for a Savior. Believe that Jesus died for your sins and rose again.

2. **Repent and Turn to God**

    o **Scripture:** *"Repent ye therefore, and be converted, that your sins may be blotted out"* (Acts 3:19).

    o **Application:** Repentance is more than feeling sorry for sin; it is a change of heart and direction.

3. **Accept Jesus as Lord**

    o **Scripture:** *"But as many as received him, to them gave he power to become the sons of God, even to them that believe on his name"* (John 1:12).

    o **Action Step:** Invite Jesus to be Lord of your life. Yield your will to His and walk in obedience to His Word.

5: Wisdom Keys and Practical Application

- **Wisdom Keys:**

    1. Forgiveness is a gift, not something we earn.
    2. Jesus' sacrifice is sufficient to cover every sin.
    3. Faith in Christ brings freedom from condemnation and a new identity.

- **Practical Steps:**

    1. Regularly confess your sins to God and receive His forgiveness (1 John 1:9).
    2. Meditate on Scriptures about forgiveness and freedom in Christ.

3. Share your testimony of forgiveness with others, pointing them to Jesus.

Closing Reflection and Prayer

Forgiveness is the foundation of our relationship with God. Jesus paid the ultimate price for our sins so that we could be reconciled to the Father. You don't have to live under the weight of guilt and shame. By believing in the finished work of Christ, you can experience true freedom and walk confidently in His mercy.

Prayer of Salvation:

Heavenly Father,

I acknowledge that I am a sinner in need of Your mercy. I believe that Jesus died on the cross for my sins and rose again on the third day. I confess Him as my Lord and Savior. Thank You for forgiving me and making me Your child. Help me to walk in the freedom and victory of Your forgiveness. In Jesus' name, Amen.

Chapter 14:

"Ask, and It Shall Be Given": Bold Faith in Prayer

An Invitation to Boldness in Prayer

In Matthew 7:7-8, Jesus offers an open invitation to every believer: *"Ask, and it shall be given you; seek, and ye shall find; knock, and it shall be opened unto you. For every one that asketh receiveth; and he that seeketh findeth; and to him that knocketh it shall be opened."* These words carry immense power and promise.

Prayer is not simply speaking words into the air; it is a divine exchange where faith touches the heart of God. Jesus assures us that our Father in Heaven hears us, desires to bless us, and delights in meeting our needs. However, effective prayer requires faith—a confident trust that God has already provided the answer in the spiritual realm before it manifests in the physical realm.

This chapter will explore the principles behind *asking, seeking, and knocking* as acts of faith, highlighting how God's will and promises are central to answered prayer. Through biblical examples, practical steps, and a prayer of supplication, you'll learn how to pray boldly and effectively.

1: Faith is the Foundation of Prayer

1. **The Faith Connection**

    Jesus emphasized that faith is the key to receiving from God. In Mark 11:24, He declared, *"Therefore I say unto you, What things soever ye desire, when ye pray, believe that ye receive them, and ye shall have them."* Faith is not wishful thinking; it is the confident assurance that God has heard your prayer and is already working on your behalf.

- **Theological Insight:** Hebrews 11:6 teaches that *"without faith it is impossible to please him: for he that cometh to God must believe that he is, and that he is a rewarder of them that diligently seek him."* Asking in faith honors God and demonstrates our dependence on His power and goodness.

2. **Illustration: The Woman with the Issue of Blood**

In Mark 5:25-34, a woman suffering from a debilitating illness for 12 years reached out to touch the hem of Jesus' garment, believing she would be healed. Her faith drew power from Jesus, and He commended her, saying, *"Daughter, thy faith hath made thee whole."* This story reminds us that faith activates God's provision.

2: Understanding God's Will in Prayer

1. **Aligning with God's Promises**

Bold prayers are rooted in the Word of God. As believers, we must pray according to His will, which is revealed in Scripture. 1 John 5:14 assures us: *"And this is the confidence that we have in him, that, if we ask any thing according to his will, he heareth us."*

- **Example from Scripture:** In 1 Kings 18:36-39, Elijah prayed boldly for God to send fire from heaven to demonstrate His power. Elijah's prayer aligned with God's will to reveal Himself to Israel, and the fire fell, turning the hearts of the people back to God.

2. **God's Good Pleasure**

Jesus describes the Father's heart in Matthew 7:11: *"If ye then, being evil, know how to give good gifts unto your children, how much more shall your Father which is in heaven give good things to them that ask him?"* God is not reluctant to bless us; He is eager to provide for His children.

3: Asking, Seeking, and Knocking in Faith

1. **The Process of Asking**

Asking is the first step in prayer. It requires humility and an acknowledgment of our dependence on God. James 4:2 says, *"Ye have not, because ye ask not."*

- o **Application:** Be specific in your requests. Instead of vague prayers, bring detailed petitions before God.

2. **The Persistence of Seeking**

Seeking implies desire and persistence. It is not enough to ask once and walk away; we must seek God's face continually. Hebrews 4:16 encourages us: *"Let us therefore come boldly unto the throne of grace, that we may obtain mercy, and find grace to help in time of need."*

- **Illustration:** In Luke 11:5-10, Jesus shares the parable of a man who persistently knocked on his friend's door at midnight, asking for bread. Because of his persistence, the man received what he asked for.

3. **The Boldness of Knocking**

   Knocking symbolizes perseverance. Sometimes, answers to prayer require spiritual warfare, as seen in Daniel 10:12-13, where Daniel's prayer was delayed by opposition in the heavenly realms. Keep knocking, trusting that God's timing is perfect.

4: The Spiritual Realm and Manifestation

1. **Believing Before Seeing**

   Jesus taught in Matthew 21:22: *"And all things, whatsoever ye shall ask in prayer, believing, ye shall receive."* The answer to your prayer exists in the spiritual realm before it becomes visible in the physical realm.

   - **Illustration:** Abraham believed God's promise of a son even when it seemed impossible. His faith was counted as righteousness (Romans 4:20-22).

2. **Speaking Faith-Filled Words**

   Faith-filled prayer involves declaring God's promises. Proverbs 18:21 reminds us, *"Death and life are in the power of the tongue."* Speak life over your situation and trust God to bring His Word to pass.

5: Practical Steps to Effective Prayer

1. **Steps to Bold Prayer:**
   - **Step 1:** Start with thanksgiving, acknowledging God's faithfulness.
   - **Step 2:** Ask specifically, aligning your request with Scripture.
   - **Step 3:** Believe that you have received the answer, even if it is not yet visible.
   - **Step 4:** Declare God's promises over your situation.
   - **Step 5:** Persist in prayer, trusting God's timing.

2. **Wisdom Keys for Prayer:**
   - Faith is essential to receive from God.
   - God's Word is the foundation of effective prayer.
   - Persistence demonstrates trust in God's goodness.

6: A Sample Prayer of Supplication

Heavenly Father,

I come to You with a heart full of faith, trusting in Your promises. Your Word says that if I ask, it will be given, and if I seek, I will find. Lord, I bring my request before You today, believing that You hear me and that You delight in blessing Your children. I declare that Your will shall be done in my life, and I thank You in advance for the answer that is already mine in the spiritual realm.

Help me to persist in faith, knowing that Your timing is perfect. In Jesus' name, Amen.

Conclusion: The Confidence of Bold Faith

Jesus' words, *"Ask, and it shall be given,"* remind us that prayer is not a last resort but a powerful privilege. As believers, we are called to approach God with confidence, rooted in His Word and faithfulness. The answers to your prayers are already prepared in the spiritual realm; your role is to believe, persist, and trust in His perfect plan.

Let us live in the confidence that our Father in Heaven is both able and willing to bless us abundantly as we boldly ask, seek, and knock.

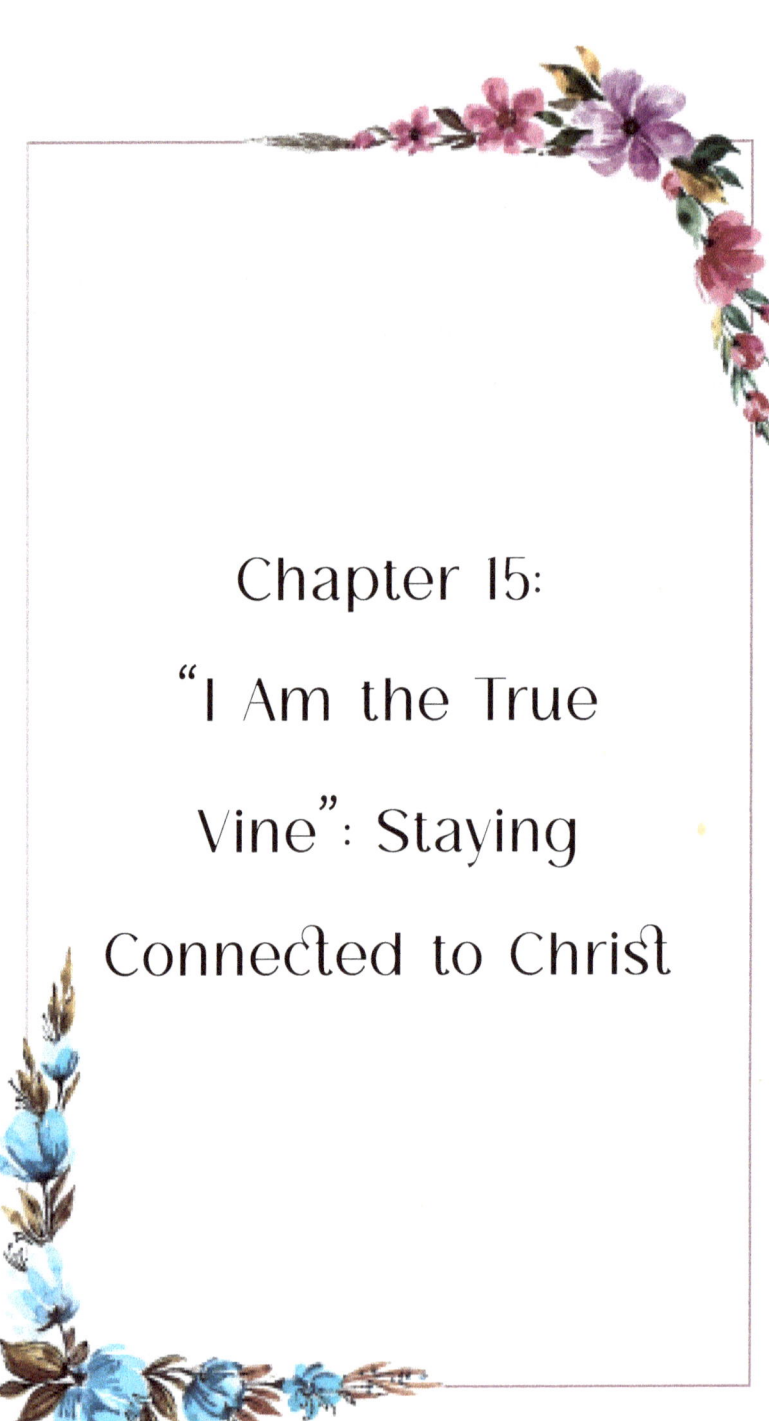

Chapter 15:

"I Am the True Vine": Staying Connected to Christ

The Life-Giving Vine

In John 15:1-5, Jesus delivers a powerful declaration: *"I am the true vine, and my Father is the husbandman... Abide in me, and I in you. As the branch cannot bear fruit of itself, except it abide in the vine; no more can ye, except ye abide in me"* (John 15:1, 4 KJV).

Through this analogy, Jesus reveals a profound truth about the Christian life: just as a branch cannot survive or bear fruit apart from the vine, we cannot thrive spiritually unless we remain connected to Him. The purpose of this chapter is to stress our responsibility to abide in Christ, explain the eternal benefits of this relationship, and outline practical ways to nurture our daily connection to Him.

1: The Necessity of Remaining in the Vine

1. **The Source of Life**

    Jesus declares Himself to be the "true vine," emphasizing that all spiritual nourishment, strength, and vitality flow from Him. Without Him, we wither. In John 15:6, He warns: *"If a man abide not in me, he is cast forth as a branch, and is withered."* This stark imagery highlights the spiritual lifelessness that comes from disconnection.

    - **Theological Theme: Dependency on Christ**

        Our spiritual life originates in Christ, who is the source of our salvation and the sustainer of our faith. Just as a vine feeds and supports its branches, Jesus provides the grace and power we need to live a fruitful life.

2. **Eternal Benefits of Connection**

   The connection to the vine is not just for this life; it has eternal implications. Abiding in Christ means that His life flows through us, preparing us for eternity. Revelation 22:14 promises: *"Blessed are they that do his commandments, that they may have right to the tree of life, and may enter in through the gates into the city."*

3. **Illustration: A Farmer's Vineyard**

   Consider a vineyard carefully tended by a farmer. Each branch must remain attached to the vine to produce grapes. A severed branch cannot sustain itself. Similarly, we must stay connected to Jesus to bear fruit, both in this life and for eternity.

2: The Life-Giving Benefits of Abiding in Christ

1. **Spiritual Fruitfulness** Jesus promises that those who abide in Him will bear much fruit. This fruit manifests as the qualities of the Spirit—*"love, joy, peace, longsuffering, gentleness, goodness, faith, meekness, temperance"* (Galatians 5:22-23 KJV)—and as actions that glorify God and bless others.

   o **Biblical Example: Paul's Ministry**

   Paul's life is a testimony to the power of abiding in Christ. Though persecuted, he was filled with joy, peace, and purpose, bearing fruit through his missionary work.

2. **Answered Prayers**

   Jesus assures us in John 15:7: *"If ye abide in me, and my words abide in you, ye shall ask what ye will, and it shall be done unto you."* When we remain connected to Him, our prayers align with His will, and we see His promises fulfilled.

3. **God's Sustaining Presence**

   In times of trial, the presence of Jesus sustains and strengthens us. Psalm 46:1 reminds us: *"God is our refuge and strength, a very present help in trouble."*

   o **Illustration: The Vine in the Storm** During a storm, the branches of a vine may sway and bend, but they remain attached and draw strength from the vine. In the same way, abiding in Christ provides stability and nourishment during life's storms.

3: Our Responsibility to Stay Connected

1. **Abiding Requires Intentionality**

   Staying connected to Jesus is not automatic. It requires intentional effort, much like maintaining any meaningful relationship. Abiding in Christ involves a commitment to prioritize Him daily.

2. **Investing Time in the Relationship**

   o **Prayer:** Spend time daily in honest, heartfelt conversation with God. Philippians 4:6 encourages: *"In* *every thing by prayer and supplication with thanksgiving let your requests be made known unto God."*

- **Scripture Reading:** Feed your spirit with God's Word. Psalm 119:105 declares: *"Thy word is a lamp unto my feet, and a light unto my path."*
- **Worship:** Worship draws us closer to the heart of God, aligning our spirits with His presence.

3. **Wisdom Keys for Abiding**

- Make time for Jesus daily, even when life gets busy.
- Let His Word guide your thoughts and decisions.
- Trust in His promises, even when answers seem delayed.

4: Practical Steps to Stay Connected

1. **Establish Daily Habits**

- Begin each day with prayer and Bible reading.
- Reflect on Scripture throughout the day.
- End the day with thanksgiving and prayer for guidance.

2. **Join a Community of Believers**

Fellowship strengthens our connection to Jesus. Hebrews 10:25 urges: *"Not forsaking the assembling of ourselves together."*

3. **Practice Obedience**

Abiding in Christ means walking in His ways. John 14:15 reminds us: *"If ye love me, keep my commandments."*

4. **Bullet Points for Connection:**
   - Start a prayer journal to document your prayers and answers.
   - Memorize a new Bible verse each week.
   - Dedicate specific times for uninterrupted worship.

5: The Danger of Disconnection

1. **The Withering Effect**

   When a branch is cut off, it withers and dies. Jesus warns in John 15:6: *"Men gather them, and cast them into the fire, and they are burned."* This illustrates the consequences of spiritual neglect.

2. **A Call to Return**

   If you have drifted from Jesus, it is never too late to reconnect. His arms are open wide, ready to restore and renew. Isaiah 55:7 promises: *"Let the wicked forsake his way... and he will have mercy upon him."*

6: A Prayer of Supplication

Heavenly Father,

Thank You for sending Jesus, the True Vine, to be our source of life and strength. I confess my need for Him and commit to abiding in Him daily. Help me to remain connected through prayer, Your Word, and worship. Let my life bear fruit that glorifies You. Draw me closer to Your heart and guide me in Your ways. In Jesus' name, Amen.

Conclusion: The Eternal Joy of Abiding

Staying connected to Christ is not a burden—it is the greatest privilege. As we abide in Him, we experience the joy of His presence, the assurance of His promises, and the hope of eternal life. Let us commit to nurturing our relationship with Him daily, trusting that He will provide all we need to bear fruit that remains.

The beauty of abiding in Christ is that it transforms every aspect of our lives. Our faith becomes stronger, our hearts grow more compassionate, and our purpose becomes clear. Staying connected to Jesus enables us to live victoriously, shining His light in a dark world. The closer we walk with Him, the more His life flows through us, producing fruit that blesses others and glorifies the Father.

So today, let this truth resonate deeply in your heart: *"I am the vine, ye are the branches"* (John 15:5). You are never alone, never powerless, and never without hope because you are connected to the Source of all life. No matter the challenges you face, His sustaining presence will carry you. Abide in Him, and He will abide in you—now and forever.

www.ingramcontent.com/pod-product-compliance
Lightning Source LLC
Chambersburg PA
CBHW060841050426
42453CB00008B/781